EIGHT LINES AND UNDER

Eight Lines and Under

An Anthology of Short, Short Poems

Edited by William Cole

The Macmillan Company, NEW YORK

For permission to include material published herein, grateful acknowledgment is made to the following: JOHN ARDEN for "The Lobster Pot." ATHENEUM HOUSE, INC., for "The Husband" from *Simeon* by Donald Finkel. Copyright © 1963, 1964 by Donald Finkel. This poem first appeared in *Poetry*. ATLANTIC-LITTLE, BROWN AND COMPANY for "Between the Acts" and "The Summing-Up" from *Selected Poems 1928–1958* by Stanley Kunitz. Copyright © 1958 by Stanley Kunitz. PEGGY BENNETT for "Shut Up, I Said," "Parable," and "A Snap Judgement on the Llama." ERIC BENTLEY and SUHRKAMP VERLAG, FRANKFURT, for "The Wheel Change" by Bertolt Brecht from *Buckower Elegien*. Copyright © 1964 by Stefan S. Brecht. This translation Copyright © 1967 by Eric Bentley. By permission of the translator and Miss Joan Daves, agent to the German publisher. PAUL BLACKBURN for "The Yawn" and "The Routine." "The Routine" was first published in *The Nation*. ANTHONY BLOND, LTD., for "Song for Mother's Day" from *The Worst Unsaid* by T. S. Matthews. ROBERT BLY for "Driving to Town Late to Mail a Letter," reprinted from *Silence in the Snowy Fields*, Wesleyan University Press, 1963. Copyright 1963 by Robert Bly. BRANDT AND BRANDT for "The General" by Siegfried Sassoon, reprinted from *Collected Poems*, published by E. P. Dutton. Copyright 1918 by Siegfried Sassoon. CAMBRIDGE UNIVERSITY PRESS for "The Single Woman"

3,886

from *Poems in Places*. HOUGHTON MIFFLIN COMPANY for "In the Museum" from *Birthdays from the Ocean* by Isabella Gardner. "In a Parlor Containing a Table" from *What a Kingdom It Was* by Galway Kinnell. "Cedar Waxwing" from *Water Ouzel* by William H. Matchett. R. G. HOWARTH for "On a Row of Nuns in a Cemetery," published in *The Penguin Book of Australian Verse*. INDIANA UNIVERSITY PRESS for "Thaw" from *The Reckless Spenders* by Walker Gibson. "The Halt" from *Prefabrications* by Josephine Miles. MRS. RANDALL JARRELL for "Death of the Ball Turret Gunner" from *Selected Poems* by Randall Jarrell. MARGOT JOHNSON AGENCY, 405 East 54th Street, New York, N.Y. 10022 for "Political Reflection" from *Mirrors and Windows* by Howard Nemerov. © 1958 by Howard Nemerov. "Absent-Minded Professor" from *New and Selected Poems* by Howard Nemerov. © 1960 by The University of Chicago. Reprinted by permission of the author's agent, Margot Johnson Agency. RICHARD KELL for "Memorandum for Minos" from *Six Irish Poets*, published by Oxford University Press. X. J. KENNEDY and THE NEW YORK TIMES for "One A.M." by X. J. Kennedy from *The New York Times*, May 11, 1962. © 1962 by The New York Times Company. GALWAY KINNELL for "Spring Oak" from *New Poems by American Poets*, Volume I, published by Ballantine Books. Copyright © 1955 by Galway Kinnell. THOMAS KINSELLA and THE DOLMEN PRESS LIMITED for "An Old Atheist Pauses by the Sea" from *Six Irish Poets* by Thomas Kinsella. Copyright © by Thomas Kinsella, 1960, 1961, 1962. ALEXANDER LAING for "How Music's Made" by Dilys Laing, published in *The Carleton Miscellany*. Copyright 1963 by *The Carlton Miscellany*, copyright 1967 by Alexander Laing. LIVERIGHT PUBLISHING CORPORATION, NEW YORK, for "I burned my candle at both ends . . ." from *Poems in Praise of Practically Nothing* by Samuel Hoffenstein. Copyright © renewed, 1956, by David Hoffenstein. THE MACMILLAN COMPANY for "Morality" from *Country Without Maps* by Jean Garrigue. Copyright © Jean Garrigue, 1964. "The Leaden-Eyed" from *Collected Poems* by Vachel Lindsay. Copyright 1914 by The Macmillan Company, renewed 1942 by Elizabeth C. Lindsay. "At My Father's Grave" and "Wheesht, Wheesht" from *Collected Poems* by Hugh MacDiarmid. Copyright 1948, © 1962 by Christopher Murray Grieve. "An Inscription By The Sea" from *Collected Poems* by Edward Arlington Robinson. Copyright 1915 by Edward Arlington Robinson, renewed 1943 by Ruth Nivison. "The Crackling Twig," "Washed in Silver," and "The Wind" from *Collected Poems* by James Stephens. Copyright 1915 by The Macmillan Company, renewed 1943 by James Stephens. "A Deux" from *The Shrinking Orchestra* by William Wood. Copyright © William Wood, 1963. "A Deep-Sworn Vow," "After Long Silence," "He Thinks Evil of Those Who Have Spoken Ill of His Beloved," "The Magi," "The Spur," "Three Movements," "The Witch," and "Youth and Age," all from *Collected Poems* by William Butler Yeats. Copyright 1906, 1916, 1919, 1928, 1933 by The Macmillan Company, renewed 1934 by W. B. Yeats, renewed 1944, 1946, 1956, 1961 by Bertha Georgie Yeats. Copyright 1940 by Bertha Georgie Yeats. MACMILLAN AND

Co., Ltd., and Mr. Michael Gibson for "Henry Turnbull" from *Collected Poems 1905–1925* by W. W. Gibson. Virgil Markham for "Outwitted" from *The Shores of Happiness*, Doubleday and Company, Inc., 1915. The Marvell Press, Hessle Yorkshire, England, for "Myxomatosis" from *The Less Deceived* by Philip Larkin. Scott Meredith Literary Agency, Inc., for "Dr. Hu . . ." from *Cannibals and Christians* by Norman Mailer. Copyright © 1966 by Norman Mailer. *Cannibals and Christians* was published by The Dial Press. The poem is here reprinted by permission of the author and his agents. McClelland and Stewart for "Poem" from *Let Us Compare Mythologies* by Leonard Cohen. Ernest G. Moll for "After Reading A Book on Abnormal Psychology," first published in *The Penguin Book of Australian Verse*. John Murray Ltd., for "In a Bath Teashop" from *Collected Poems* by John Betjeman. The Nation for "By a rich fast moving stream . . ." by John Tagliabue. First published in the issue of September 19, 1966, of *The Nation*. New Directions Publishing Corporation for "Thousand-and-first Ship" from *The Crack Up* by F. Scott Fitzgerald. Copyright © 1954 by New Directions. "A Pact" and "Tame Cat" from *Personae* by Ezra Pound. Copyright © 1926, 1953 by Ezra Pound. "Advice to Young Children," "Autumn," and "Pad, Pad" from *Selected Poems* by Stevie Smith. Copyright © 1962, 1964 by Stevie Smith. "The Act" from *Collected Later Poems* by William Carlos Williams. Copyright 1944, © 1963 by William Carlos Williams. The New Statesman, London, for "A St. Cecilia's Day Epigram" by Peter Porter. Reprinted from the issue of November 20, 1964. The New Yorker Magazine, Inc., for "To A Man In a Picture Window Watching Television" by Mildred Weston. Copyright © 1960 The New Yorker Magazine, Inc., reprinted from the issue of December 17, 1960. The Ohio State University Press and William Dickey for "Spectrum" from *Interpreter's House* by William Dickey. Copyright © 1962, 1963 by William Dickey. All rights reserved. Used by permission of the publisher and the author. Oxford University Press, Canada, for "News of the Phoenix" from *Collected Poems* by A. J. M. Smith. Oxford University Press, London, for "The Fox Rhyme" from *The Tale of the Monster Horse* by Ian Seraillier. "A Question," "To the Oaks of Glencree," and "In Glencullen" by John M. Synge from *Synge Complete Poems*, edited by Robin Skelton. Oxford University Press, Inc., New York, for "Two Hundred Girls in Tights and Halters" from *A Little Geste and Other Poems* by Daniel G. Hoffman. Copyright © 1960 by Daniel G. Hoffman. Reprinted by permission of the publisher. "Fragment" from *Poems of Gerard Manley Hopkins*, third edition, edited by W. H. Gardner. Copyright 1948 by Oxford University Press, Inc. Reprinted by permission of the publisher. A. D. Peters & Company for "The Brewer Man" and "Old Dan'l" from *Selected Poems* by L. A. G. Strong. "Juliet," "On Mundane Acquaintances," and "On a Hand" from *Sonnets and Verse* by Hilaire Belloc, and "Grandmamma's Birthday" from *Collected Poems and Letters of Hilaire Belloc*. Ralph Pomeroy for "Trying to Sleep" from *The Canaries as They Are* by Ralph Pomeroy, published by

6

Charioteer Press. Copyright 1965 by Ralph Pomeroy. RANDOM HOUSE, INC., and ALFRED A. KNOPF, INC., for "Lord Finchley" from *Cautionary Verses* by Hilaire Belloc. Published 1941 by Alfred A. Knopf, Inc. "The Young Recruit" from *Tumultous Shore* by Arthur Davison Ficke. Copyright 1941 by Arthur Davison Ficke. Reprinted by permission of Alfred A. Knopf, Inc. "Of the Surface of Things" from *The Collected Poems of Wallace Stevens.* Copyright 1923 and renewed 1951 by Wallace Stevens. Reprinted by permission of Alfred A. Knopf, Inc. "Winter Ocean" and "Deities and Beasts" from *Telephone Poles* by John Updike. Copyright © 1960, 1959 by John Updike. Reprinted by permission of Alfred A. Knopf, Inc. "Epitaph on a Tyrant" from *The Collected Poetry of W. H. Auden.* Copyright 1940 by W. H. Auden. Reprinted by permission of Random House, Inc. "On Lavater's Song of a Christian to Christ" from *Twenty German Poets* edited by Walter Kaufman. Copyright © 1962 by Random House, Inc. "Eagle Valor, Chicken Mind" from *Double Axe and Other Poems* by Robinson Jeffers. Copyright 1948 by Robinson Jeffers. Reprinted by permission of Random House, Inc. "Cremation" from *Beginning and the End and Other Poems* by Robinson Jeffers. Copyright © 1963 by Garth Jeffers and Donnan Jeffers. Reprinted by permission of Random House, Inc. "As bad as a Mile" and "Take one Home for the Kiddies" from *The Whitsun Weddings* by Philip Larkin. Copyright © 1960, 1964 by Philip Larkin. Reprinted by permission of Random House, Inc. THE BEN ROTH AGENCY for "In a Town Garden" by Donald Mattam, "Open to Visitors" by E. V. Milner, "A Word of Encouragement" by J. R. Pope, and "La Carte" by Justin Richardson, all from *Punch.* © Punch Publications Ltd. ROUTLEDGE AND KEGAN PAUL for "The Embankment" from *Speculations* by T. E. Hulme. THE RYERSON PRESS, Toronto, for "A Bed Without a Woman," "The Bottle of Chianti," and "Search" from *The Colour of the Times* by Raymond Souster. KENNETH A. SCHWARTZ for "What curious dresses all men wear . . ." by Delmore Schwartz, from an article by Dwight Macdonald in *The New York Review of Books.* CHARLES SCRIBNER'S SONS for "Like They Say" from *For Love* by Robert Creeley. Copyright © 1962 Robert Creeley. "Then wear the gold hat . . ." from *The Great Gatsby* by F. Scott Fitzgerald. Copyright 1925 Charles Scribner's Sons, renewal copyright 1953 Frances Scott Fitzgerald Lanahan. "When Adam day by day . . ." and "The stars have not dealt . . ." by A. E. Housman from *My Brother, A. E. Housman* by Laurence Housman. Copyright 1937, 1938 Laurence Housman, renewal copyright © 1965, 1966 Lloyds Bank Limited. SHEL SILVERSTEIN for "Guess what I have gone and done . . .," "In that dark cave . . .," and "Tell me just the miraculi . . ." MICHAEL SILVERTON for "Life in the Country" from *Battery Park* by Michael Silverton, published by Thing Press, 1966. JOHN SIMON for "Ameinias." THE SIXTIES PRESS for "I am a Sioux Brave . . ." by James Wright, originally printed in *The Sixties,* No. 8, p. 79. "Walnut" by Jorge Carrera Andrade, translated by Philip Silver, originally printed in *The Sixties,* No. 7, p. 39. "Snow" by John Kelleher, originally printed in *The*

Sixties, No. 7, p. 39. W. D. SNODGRASS and POETRY for "Junker Schmidt" by Kozma Prutkov, translated by W. D. Snodgrass and Tanya Tolstoy from *Poetry*, July 1964. THE SOCIETY OF AUTHORS for "Lines from *Winged Chariot*" by Walter de la Mare. Used by permission of The Literary Trustees of Walter de la Mare and The Society of Authors as their representative. THE SPECTATOR for "War Story" by Jon Stallworthy, which appeared in *The Spectator* of March 8, 1963, and is reproduced by permission. ALAN SWALLOW, PUBLISHER, for "To the Contemporary Muse" from *The Astronomers* by Edgar Bowers. Copyright 1965 by Edgar Bowers. Reprinted by permission of the publisher. "Epitaph," "Epigram," and "This Humanist whom no beliefs constrained . . ." from *The Exclusion of a Rhyme: Poems and Epigrams* by J. V. Cunningham. Copyright 1960 by J. V. Cunningham. Reprinted by permission of the publisher. "Nescir vox missa reverti . . ." from *To What Strangers, What Welcome* by J. V. Cunningham. Copyright 1964 by J. V. Cunningham. Reprinted by permission of the publisher. "Picture Framing" from *Early Rain* by Bert Meyers. Copyright 1960 by Bert Meyers. Reprinted by permission of the publisher. "April" from *Collected Poems* by Yvor Winters. Copyright 1952, 1960 by Yvor Winters. Reprinted by permission of the publisher. ROBERT SWARD for "Nightgown, Wife's Gown," "Pet Shop," and "Proposal" from *Kissing the Dancer* by Robert Sward, Cornell University Press. Copyright © 1960, 1961, 1962, 1963, 1964 by Robert Sward. Reprinted by permission of the author. THE UNIVERSITY OF CALIFORNIA PRESS for "Korf's Joke" by Christian Morgenstern, translated by Max Knight, from *Galgenlieder* by Christian Morgenstern. THE UNIVERSITY OF CHICAGO PRESS for "Letter from Slough Pond" from *The Looking Glass* by Isabella Gardner. Copyright © 1961 by The University of Chicago. THE UNIVERSITY OF PITTSBURGH PRESS for "God and Man" from *My Sons to God* by Samuel Hazo. Copyright 1965 by Samuel Hazo. THE VIKING PRESS, INC., for "For Anne" and "I Wonder How Many People in This City" from *The Spice-Box of Earth* by Leonard Cohen. Copyright 1961 in all countries of the International Copyright Union by McClelland and Stewart Ltd., Toronto, all rights reserved. "Discord in Childhood" and "Green" from *The Complete Poems of D. H. Lawrence*, edited by Vivian de Sola Pinto and F. Warren Roberts. Copyright 1920 by B. W. Huebsch, Inc., 1947 by Frieda Lawrence, all rights reserved. "I May, I Might, I Must" from *A Marianne Moore Reader* by Marianne Moore. Copyright 1959 by Marianne Moore. All rights reserved. WESLEYAN UNIVERSITY PRESS for "American Poetry," "In the Suburbs," and "Birch" from *At the End of the Open Road* by Louis Simpson. Copyright © 1963 by Louis Simpson. "Blue Jay" from *The Orb Weaver* by Robert Francis. Copyright © 1959 by Robert Francis. "The Beautiful" and "To the Wind at Morn" from *The Complete Poems Of W. H. Davies*. Copyright © 1963 by Jonathan Cape Limited.

Contents

Introduction

THESE poems are all eight lines and under, except once in a while I cheat. When tempted by an occasional magnificent nine- or ten-line poem, I succumbed.

Unbeknownst to themselves, three contemporary poets started this: George Barker, Leonard Cohen, and J. V. Cunningham. They were contributors to a quirky anthology, *Poet's Choice*, in which some hundred poets each chose a favorite and representative poem of his own, and said why. Ask a poet to pick a favorite poem of his own for publication, and you can bet he'll pick a long one; it will also be a complicated one. His explanation of the whys and wherefores will be longer and yet more obscure. This is known as the Best Foot Forward theory. Given this opportunity to exhibit their fancy work on the high wire, Messrs. Barker, Cohen, and Cunningham chose poems of four and six lines, and appended terse commentary. This set me to thinking about the beauty of brevity, and, with no ulterior anthologistic purpose, I began copying attractive short poems and stuffing them in a file. Thus, over five years, this anthology accreted.

The short poem has never been acknowledged as a separate form of poetic endeavor. The poets in the imagist movement in London before World War I believed in a poetry that was clear, economical, and written in natural speech patterns; but brevity was not a dictum. The Japanese, of course, have their short forms, notably the seventeen-syllable *haiku* and the thirty-one-syllable *tanka*. These restricting forms have always left me cold; I find myself counting syllables on my fingers, and being amazed when they come out right. Quite a trick, *haiku* and *tanka*, but, as verse forms, about as interesting as the limerick. It is quite possible that an unacknowledged seventeen- or thirty-one-syllable poem has crept into these pages, but who's counting?

A poet working in eight lines must keep himself under tight rein. Each word must pull its own load. He must keep his eye on the image, the thought, the moment of discovery. The short poem seems to be a particularly twentieth-century form. It is perhaps not coincidence that a good three-quarters of the poems in this collection are contemporary (the Index gives birth and death dates for earlier poets). Poets of the past would sometimes *create* in short units—I think particularly of Pope. W. H. Auden has pointed out in a fascinating essay on Byron that ottava rima has great structural advantages: "As a unit, eight lines gives space enough to describe a single event or elaborate upon a single idea without having to run on to the next stanza." But there are very few *complete* short poems to be found in the work of the earlier major poets.

Short should not be equated with trivial. Some of the poems treat minor subjects and are light and airy, but they are all poems, not tricks or oddities. They range from light to dark. The lightest will, I hope, be amusing or glancingly instructive. Many of the more serious will, to quote an anonymous reviewer of a book of aphorisms, give "a quick and pleasant feeling of intellectual stimulation without continued mental effort." The darkest, deepest poems are those of Yeats. His "The Magi" is, within eight lines, complex, richly textured, and can be mulled over for hours.

The poets range from half-beats to aggressively traditional; there are surprises for everyone. I am particularly pleased to print a number of poems by three undervalued English poets: Frances Cornford, Andrew Young, and R. S. Thomas. The poems of Scott Fitzgerald are seldom seen, and I'm sure this is the first book publication of Delmore Schwartz's superb "What curious dresses all men wear," which he had inscribed to Dwight Macdonald in a volume of his poems. My only disappointment has been that the intransigency of their publisher has forced me to leave out poems by Louise Bogan and Robert Lowell.

This anthology is not trying to prove anything about trends, schools, or movements; it is simply claiming, "Here are a couple of hundred short, short poems, each of which has amused, amazed, or excited the compiler." To say more would be to bring suspicion on my praise of brevity. The last word is Alexander Pope's:

> Words are like leaves; and where they most abound,
> Much fruit of sense beneath is rarely found.

WILLIAM COLE

I

"And that's the way
The kissing goes."

A Deux

I TWIST your arm,
You twist my leg,
I make you cry,
You make me beg,
I dry your eyes,
You wipe my nose,
And that's the way
The kissing goes.

William Wood

For Anne

WITH Annie gone
Whose eyes to compare
With the morning sun?

Not that I did compare,
But I do compare
Now that she's gone.

Leonard Cohen

A Deep-Sworn Vow

OTHERS because you did not keep
That deep-sworn vow have been friends of mine;
Yet always when I look death in the face,
When I clamber to the heights of sleep,
Or when I grow excited with wine,
Suddenly I meet your face.

W. B. Yeats

The Corner of the Field

HERE the young lover, on his elbow raised,
Looked at his happy girl with grass surrounded,
And flicked the spotted beetle from her wrist:
She, with head thrown back, at heaven gazed,
At Suffolk clouds, serene and slow and mounded;
Then calmly smiled at him before they kissed.

Frances Cornford

Nightgown, Wife's Gown

WHERE do people go when they go to sleep?
I envy them. I want to go there too.
I am outside of them, married to them.
Nightgown, wife's gown, women that you look at,
Beside them—I knock on their shoulder blades
Ask to be let in. It is forbidden.
But you're my wife, I say. There is no reply.
Arms around her, I caress her wings.

Robert Sward

All This Sunday Long

ALL this Sunday long it has snowed,
and I weighted with the old grief
struggling to unseat her from my mind.

Yet winnowing our past I cannot find
a snow-gilded scene however brief:
thus do I wilfully increase my load.

B. S. Johnson

Sea Love

TIDE be runnin' the great world over:
    'Twas only last June month I mind that we
Was thinkin' the toss and the call in the breast of
        the lover
    So everlastin' as the sea.

Here's the same little fishes that sputter and swim,
    Wi' the moon's old glim on the gray, wet sand;
An' him no more to me nor me to him
    Than the wind goin' over my hand.

Charlotte Mew

In a Bath Teashop

"LET us now speak, for the love we bear one another—
    Let us hold hands and look."
She, such a very ordinary little woman;
    He, such a thumping crook;
But both, for a moment, little lower than the angels
    In the teashop's ingle-nook.

John Betjeman

Ivy and Holly

ANCIENTLY in this village,
As true as tale of Troy,
The boys would burn an ivy girl,
The girls a holly boy.

Prickly am I as holly,
Raven as ivy you;
The village burns us on its tongue,
And all the tale is true.

E. H. W. Meyerstein

"He Knoweth Not that the Dead Are Thine"

THE weapon that you fought with was a word,
And with that word you stabbed me to the heart.
Not once but twice you did it, for the sword
　　Made no blood start.

They have not tried you for your life. You go
Strong in such innocence as men will boast.
They have not buried me. They do not know
　　Life from its ghost.

Mary Coleridge

Letter from Slough Pond

HERE where you left me alone
the soft wind sighs through my wishbone
the sun is lapping at my flesh
I couple with the ripples of the fresh
pond water. I am rolled by the roiling sea.
Love, in our wide bed, do you lie lonely?
The spoon of longing stirs my marrow
and I thank God this bed is narrow.

Isabella Gardner

Wheesht, Wheesht

WHEESHT, wheesht, my foolish hert,
For weel ye ken
I widna ha'e ye stert
Auld ploys again.

It's guid to see her lie
Sae snod an' cool,
A' lust o' loving' by—
Wheesht, wheesht, ye fule!

Hugh MacDiarmid

---

snod—cozy, snug

Reproach to Julia

JULIA, how Irishly you sacrifice
Love to pity, pity to ill-humor,
Yourself to love, still haggling at the price.

Robert Graves

Penal Law

BURN Ovid with the rest. Lovers will find
A hedge-school for themselves and learn by heart
All that the clergy banish from the mind,
When hands are joined and head bows in the dark.

Austin Clarke

On a Hand

HER hand which touched my hand she moved away,
But there it lies, for ever and a day.

Hilaire Belloc

"And that's the way the kissing goes."   13

The Brewer's Man

HAVE I a wife? Bedam I have!
    But we was badly mated:
I hit her a great clout one night,
    And now we're separated.

And mornin's, going to my work,
    I meets her on the quay:
"Good mornin' to ye, ma'am," says I;
    "To hell with ye," says she.

L. A. G. Strong

Before the Barn-Door Crowing

BEFORE the barn-door crowing,
    The cock by hens attended,
His eyes around him throwing,
    Stands for a while suspended:
Then one he singles from the crew,
    And cheers the happy hen;
With how do you do, and how do you do,
    And how do you do again.

John Gay

From a Woman to a Greedy Lover

WHAT is this recompense you'd have from me?
Melville asked no compassion of the sea.
Roll to and fro, forgotten in my rack,
Love as you please—I owe you nothing back.

Norman Cameron

Evening Star

EVENING Star, enemy of lovers, why
Do you move so slowly across the sky
Now that another lover
Is warm under Maisie's bedcover?

George Barker

Epigram

YOU ask me how Contempt who claims to sleep
With every woman that has ever been
Can still maintain that women are skin deep?
They never let him any deeper in.

J. V. Cunningham

"And that's the way the kissing goes." 15

We're a' Dry wi' the Drinkin' O't

WE'RE a' dry wi' the drinkin' o't,
    We're a' dry wi' the drinkin' o't,
The minister kissed the fiddler's wife,
    And he couldna preach for thinkin' o't.

Anonymous

Why Do We Lie

"Why do we lie," she questioned, her warm eyes
on the grey Autumn wind and its coursing,
"all afternoon wasted in a bed like this?"
"Because we cannot lie all night together."
"Yes," she said, satisfied at my reasoning,
but going on to search her cruel mind
for better excuses to leave my narrow bed.

B. S. Johnson

Lines Supposed To Have Been Addressed to Fanny Brawne

THIS living hand, now warm and capable
Of earnest grasping, would, if it were cold
And in the icy silence of the tomb,
So haunt thy days and chill thy dreaming nights
That thou would[st] wish thine own heart dry of blood
So in my veins red life might stream again,
And thou be conscience-calm'd—see here it is—
I hold it towards you.

John Keats

Life in the Country

I PERCEIVE the cow's slightly
Changed expression. I am reminded
To tell you that your eyelid
Quivers when you whisper in my ear,
& that when you whisper in my ear,
      the cow seems embarrassed,
Averts her head
      & stops chewing.

Michael Silverton

"And that's the way the kissing goes."   17

Love Without Hope

LOVE without hope, as when the young bird-catcher
Swept off his tall hat to the Squire's own daughter,
So let the imprisoned larks escape and fly
Singing about her head, as she rode by.

Robert Graves

Proposal

THREE days I dreamed her—
Four arms, four legs, humped back and blackish.
I recognize her by her limp. Taking me
By the handful, she proposes marriage.
Circular, headless, scaly
Her loveliness amazes me. My consent
Is immediate. Ladies and gentlemen, my wife.

Robert Sward

Poem

I HEARD of a man
who says words so beautifully
that if he only speaks their name
women give themselves to him.

If I am dumb beside your body
while silence blossoms like tumors on our lips
it is because I hear a man climb stairs
and clear his throat outside our door.

Leonard Cohen

The Question

LOVELY of hair and breast and face,
Utterly lost to Christian grace,
    How will you lift that bankrupt head
    When all the butterfly beauty's dead?

Norman Gale

The Guitarist Tunes Up

WITH what attentive courtesy he bent
Over his instrument;
Not as a lordly conquerer who could
Command both wire and wood,
But as a man with a loved woman might,
Inquiring with delight
What slight essential things she had to say
Before they started, he and she, to play.

Frances Cornford

The Question Answer'd

WHAT is it men in women do require?
The lineaments of Gratified Desire.
What is it women do in men require?
The lineaments of Gratified Desire.

William Blake

II

"The hundred-dollar cats, the sixty-
Dollar dogs; the lions, the tigers ..."

Pet Shop

THE hundred-dollar cats, the sixty-
Dollar dogs; the lions, the tigers;
The six, miniature, white, snake-eating
Fish; the snakes, the monkeys (with grins like
Gelded poodles); the parakeets, owls
Flamingos, pink pigeons and the small, headless
Proprietor, silky, creeping & jewelled.

Robert Sward

The Death of a Snake

"Death and generation are both mysteries of nature, and
somewhat resemble each other."—Marcus Aurelius

BRUISED by a heel he strove to die,
In frantic spirals bored the air,
Turned his pale belly uponward to the sky
In coitus with death: and here and there
Scored in the dust quick ideographs of pain—
These, that the wind removed, in memory remain.

William Plomer

January

THE fox drags its wounded belly
Over the snow, the crimson seeds
Of blood burst with a mild explosion,
Soft as excrement, bold as roses.

Over the snow that feels no pity,
Whose white hands can give no healing,
The fox drags its wounded belly.

R. S. Thomas

In Glencullen

THRUSH, linnet, stare and wren,
Brown lark beside the sun,
Take thought of kestrel, sparrow-hawk,
Birdlime and roving gun.

You great-great-grandchildren
Of birds I've listened to,
I think I robbed your ancestors
When I was young as you.

John Millington Synge

Birds at Winter Nightfall

(*triolet*)

AROUND the house the flakes fly faster,
And all the berries now are gone
From holly and cotoneaster
Around the house. The flakes fly!—faster
Shutting indoors that crumb-outcaster
We used to see upon the lawn
Around the house. The flakes fly faster,
And all the berries now are gone!

Thomas Hardy

The Lobster Pot

WHO can tell how the lobster got
Into the lobster pot?
When he went in he did not doubt
There was a passage out.
There was not.

John Arden

Fragment

REPEAT that, repeat,
Cuckoo, bird, and open ear wells, heart-springs, delightfully
    sweet,
With a ballad, with a ballad, a rebound
Off trundled timber and scoops of the hillside ground,
          hollow hollow hollow ground:
The whole landscape flushes on a sudden at a sound.

Gerard Manley Hopkins

Deities and Beasts

TALL Atlas, Jupiter, Hercules, Thor,
Just like the antic pagan gods of yore,
Make up a too-erratic pantheon
For mortal men to be dependent on.

I much prefer, myself, the humble RAT,
The tiny Terrier, the short Hawk that
Makes secret flight, and the Sparrow, whose fall
Is never mentioned in the press at all.

John Updike

Pussycat Sits on a Chair

PUSSYCAT sits on a chair
Implacably with acid stare.

Those who early loved in vain
Use the cat to try again,

And test their bruised omnipotence
Against the cat's austere defense.

Edward Newman Horn

Life

I MET four guinea hens today,
creaking like pulleys.

"a crrk," said one,
"a crrk," said two,
"a crrk," said three,
"a crrk," said four.

I agree with you cheerfully, ladies.

Alfred Kreymborg

Questioning Faces

THE winter owl banked just in time to pass
And save herself from breaking window glass.
And her wings straining suddenly aspread
Caught color from the last of evening red
In a display of underdown and quill
To glassed-in children at the window sill.

Robert Frost

The Fox Rhyme

AUNT was on the garden seat
    Enjoying a wee nap and
Along came a fox! teeth
    Closed with a snap and
He's running to the woods with her
    A-dangle and a-flap and—
Run, uncle, run
    And see what has happened!

Ian Serraillier

The View from Here

IN Antarctica drooping their little shoulders
like bottles the penguins stand, small,
sad, black—and the wind
bites hard over them.

Edging the continent they huddle to turn their eyes.
Penguins, we can't help you; and all that cold
hangs over us too, wide beyond thought.
We too stand and wait.

William Stafford

Like They Say

UNDERNEATH the tree on some
soft grass I sat, I

watched two happy
woodpeckers be dis-

turbed by my presence. And
why not, I thought to

myself, why
not.

Robert Creeley

Myxomatosis

CAUGHT in the centre of a soundless field
While hot inexplicable hours go by
What trap is this? Where were its teeth concealed?
You seem to ask.
        I make a sharp reply,
Then clean my stick. I'm glad I can't explain
Just in what jaws you were to suppurate:
You may have thought things would come right again
If you could only keep still and wait.

Philip Larkin

The Eagle

HE hangs between his wings outspread
    Level and still
And bends a narrow golden head,
    Scanning the ground to kill.

Yet as he sails and smoothly swings
    Round the hill-side,
He looks as though from his own wings
    He hung down crucified.

Andrew Young

April

THE little goat
crops
new grass lying down
leaps up eight inches
into air and
lands on four feet.
Not a tremor—
solid in the
spring and serious
he walks away.

Yvor Winters

Cedar Waxwing

DRUNK on sour cherries, the harlequin of birds
Lurches through the branches and lisps in bleared content,
While a Temperance Union Catbird shrieks her words
In a scathing, scolding lecture he's too happy to resent.

William H. Matchett

THE tiger stalking in the night
Is tremulous, half dead with fright.

Edward Newman Horn

Philological

THE British puss demurely mews;
His transatlantic kin meow.
The kine in Minnesota moo;
Not so the gentle Devon cows:
      They low,
As every school child ought to know.

John Updike

A Snap Judgement on the Llama

THE Llama seems a sensitive creature,
Quiet and aloof, shy, discreet;
Her neck seems a bit long, as a leg is long,
But she has slender ankles and dainty feet—
And gazes on her present strange fortunes
With many a delicate sniff,
Her quickfingered hare-nose wiggling constantly
As if being nibbled inward by its own self.

Peggy Bennett

The Woodman's Dog

SHAGGY, and lean, and shrewd, with pointed ears
And tail cropped short, half lurcher and half cur—
His dog attends him. Close behind his heel
Now creeps he slow; and now with many a frisk
Wild-scampering, snatches up the drifted snow
With ivory teeth, or plows it with his snout;
Then shakes his powdered coat and barks for joy.

William Cowper

Blue Jay

So bandit-eyed, so undovelike a bird
to be my pastoral father's favorite—
skulker and blusterer
whose every arrival is a raid.

Love made the bird no gentler
nor him who loved less gentle.
Still, still the wild blue feather
brings my mild father.

Robert Francis

III

"So he said then:
I will make the poem ..."

The Maker

So he said then: I will make the poem,
I will make it now. He took pencil,
The mind's cartridge, and blank paper,
And drilled his thoughts to the slow beat

Of the blood's drum; and there it formed
On the white surface and went marching
Onward through time, while the spent cities
And dry hearts smoked in its wake.

R. S. Thomas

He Thinks of Those Who Have Spoken
Evil of His Beloved

HALF close your eyelids, loosen your hair,
And dream about the great and their pride;
They have spoken against you everywhere,
But weigh this song with the great and their pride;
I made it out of a mouthful of air,
Their children's children shall say they have lied.

W. B. Yeats

Night Crow

WHEN I saw that clumsy crow
Flap from a wasted tree,
A shape in the mind rose up:
Over the gulfs of dream
Flew a tremendous bird
Further and further away
Into a moonless black,
Deep in the brain, far back.

Theodore Roethke

What Curious Dresses All Men Wear

WHAT curious dresses all men wear!
The walker you met in a brown study,
The President smug in rotogravure,
The mannequin, the bathing beauty,

The bubble-dancer, the deep-sea diver,
The bureaucrat, the adulterer,
Hide private parts which I disclose
To those who know what a poem knows.

Delmore Schwartz

By a rich fast moving stream

I
saw
the
dragonfly
become a
dragon and
then a poem
about a dragonfly
becoming a dangerous
reader in fast pursuit
of summer transformations.

John Tagliabue

Who Translates a Poet Badly . . .
Mal traductor de poeta . . .

WHO translates a poet badly
Plays a lackey's role
Grotesquely garbed
In his master's clothes.

Gonzalez Prada
Translated from the Spanish
by William M. Davis

"So he said then: I will make the poem . . ."   39

The Poet's Fate

WHAT is a modern Poet's fate.
To write his thought upon a slate;
The Critic spits on what is done,
Gives it a wipe—and all is gone.

Thomas Hood

My Muse and I, Ere Youth and Spirits Fled

MY muse and I, ere youth and spirits fled,
Sat up together many a night, no doubt;
But now I've sent the poor old lass to bed,
Simply because my fire is going out.

George Colman the Younger

A Pact

I MAKE a pact with you, Walt Whitman—
I have detested you long enough.
I come to you as a grown child
Who has had a pig-headed father;
I am old enough now to make friends.
It was you that broke the new wood,
Now is a time for carving.
We have one sap and one root—
Let there be commerce between us.

Ezra Pound

Confidential

IN the poet's vigorous fifties,
With prolific good work done,
He writes yet more virile poems
Secretly. He hides them
To be published in his seventies.

Winfield Townley Scott

"So he said then: I will make the poem . . ."   41

American Poetry

WHATEVER it is, it must have
A stomach that can digest
Rubber, coal, uranium, moons, poems.

Like the shark it contains a shoe.
It must swim for miles through the desert
Uttering cries that are almost human.

Louis Simpson

The Spur

You think it horrible that lust and rage
Should dance attention upon my old age;
They were not such a plague when I was young;
What else have I to spur me into song?

W. B. Yeats

Academic

THE stethoscope tells what everyone fears:
You're likely to go on living for years,
With a nurse-maid waddle and a shop-girl simper,
And the style of your prose growing limper and limper.

Theodore Roethke

Throughout the World

THROUGHOUT the world, if it were sought,
Fair words enough a man shall find:
They be good cheap, they cost right nought,
Their substance is but only wind:
  But well to say and so to mean,
  That sweet accord is seldom seen.

Sir Thomas Wyatt

LANGUAGE has not the power to speak what love indites:
The Soul lies buried in the ink that writes.

John Clare

To the Contemporary Muse

HONESTY, little slut, must you insist
On hearing every dirty word I know
And all my worst affairs? Are impotence,
Insanity, and lying what you lust for?
Your hands are cold, feeling me in the dark.

Edgar Bowers

Sanctity

To be a poet and not know the trade,
To be a lover and repel all women;
Twin ironies by which great saints are made,
The agonising pincer-jaws of Heaven.

Patrick Kavanagh

Three Movements

SHAKESPEAREAN fish swam the sea, far away from land;
Romantic fish swam in nets coming to the hand;
What are all those fish that lie gasping on the strand?

W. B. Yeats

Of the Surface of Things

I

IN my room, the world is beyond my understanding;
But when I walk I see that it consists of three or four
 hills and a cloud.

II

From my balcony, I survey the yellow air,
Reading where I have written,
"The spring is like a belle undressing."

III

The gold tree is blue.
The singer has pulled his cloak over his head.
The moon is in the folds of the cloak.

Wallace Stevens

IV

"... a mixture of foolish and wise."

An Epitaph

A LOVELY young lady I mourn in my rhymes:
She was pleasant, good-natured and civil sometimes.
Her figure was good: she had very fine eyes,
And her talk was a mixture of foolish and wise.
Her adorers were many, and one of them said,
"She waltzed rather well! It's a pity she's dead!"

G. J. Cayley

❧

Korf's Joke

KORF invents a novel kind of joke
which won't take effect for many hours.
Everyone is bored when first he hears it.

But he will, as though a fuse were burning,
suddenly wake up in bed at night-time,
smiling sweetly like a well-fed baby.

Christian Morgenstern
Translated from the German
by Max Knight

". . . a mixture of foolish and wise."

Philander

Poetical *Philander* only thought to love:
He went to bed with what he thought the girls were symbols of.

Donald Hall

Hogamus, Higamus

HOGAMUS, higamus,
Men are polygamous;
Higamus, hogamus,
Women monogamous.

Anonymous

After Reading a Book on Abnormal Psychology

Bow all desires—even unknown ones—I had
Stand stript before me with their names writ under.
And will this make me really sane, I wonder,
Or only more intelligently mad?

Ernest G. Moll

Please Tell Me Just the Fabuli

PLEASE tell me just the fabuli,
The miraculi,
The gargantua;
And kindly, kindly spare me
All this insignifigancia.

Shel Silverstein

Epigram

MIDAS, they say, possessed the art of old
Of turning whatsoe'er he touch'd to gold;
This modern statesmen can reverse with ease—
Touch *them* with gold, *they'll turn to what you please.*

John Wolcot

The Kentucky Thoroughbred

I LOVE the hoss from hoof to head,
From head to hoof and tail to mane;
I love the hoss, as I have said,
From head to hoof and back again.

I love my God the first of all,
Then Him that perished on the Cross;
And next my wife, and then I fall
Down on my knees and love the hoss.

James Whitcomb Riley

A Word of Encouragement

O WHAT a tangled web we weave
When first we practise to deceive!
But when we've practised quite a while
How vastly we improve our style!

J. R. Pope

On Lavater's Song of a Christian to Christ

"Thou art! Thou art!!" Lavater says. "Thou art!!
Thou art!!! Thou art!!!! Thou art, Christ our Lord!!!!!"
He would not be so violent in his repetition
if it were not a questionable proposition.

> *Johann Wolfgang von Goethe*
> *Translated from the German by*
> *Walter Kaufmann*

Ameinias

OF Ameinias nothing more is known for sure
Except: he was most worthy, though quite poor.
Which may explain why he remains obscure.

> *John Simon*

On Treason

TREASON doth never prosper: what's the reason?
Why, when it prospers, none dare call it treason.

> *Sir John Harington*

". . . a mixture of foolish and wise."　　53

Sir Joshua Reynolds

WHEN Sir Joshua Reynolds died
    All nature was degraded;
The King dropped a tear into the Queen's ear,
    And all his pictures faded.

                        William Blake

On a Wag in Mauchline

LAMENT him, Mauchline husbands a',
    He aften did assist ye;
For had ye stayed whole years awa',
    Your wives they ne'er had missed ye.
Ye Mauchline bairns, as on ye pass
    To school in bands thegither,
O tread ye lightly on his grass—
    Perhaps he was your father.

                        Robert Burns

In a Town Garden

LOVELIEST of trees, the cherry now
Is hung with bloom along the bough,
As every urchin by my fence
Notes for future reference.

Donald Mattam

La Carte

IT takes much art
To choose à la carte
For less than they quote
For the table d'hôte.

Justin Richardson

Grandmamma's Birthday

DEAR Grandmamma, with what we give,
We humbly pray that you may live
For many, many happy years:
Although you bore us all to tears.

Hilaire Belloc

England

OH, England.
  Sick in head and sick in heart,
  Sick in whole and every part:
  And yet sicker thou art still
  For thinking that thou art not ill.

Anonymous
(seventeenth century)

On Marriage

How happy a thing were a wedding,
    And a bedding,
If a man might purchase a wife
    For a twelvemonth and a day;
But to live with her all a man's life,
    For ever and for aye,
Till she grow as gray as a cat,
Good faith, Mr. Parson, excuse me from that!

Thomas Flatman

❦

Wilt Thou Lend Me Thy Mare?

WILT thou lend me thy mare to go a mile?
No, she's lamed leaping over a style.
   But if thou wilt her to me spare
   Thou shalt have money for thy mare.
     O, O, say you so?
     Money will make the mare to go,
     Money will make the mare to go.

Anonymous
(eighteenth century)

Lord Finchley

LORD Finchley tried to mend the Electric Light
Himself. It struck him dead: And serve him right!
It is the business of the wealthy man
To give employment to the artisan.

Hilaire Belloc

In That Dark Cave

IN that dark cave
A lonely, burned-out dragon sits,
And sighs,
And sadly sniffs
The bone-filled suit of armor
That lies rusting at his door.

Shel Silverstein

When Adam Day by Day

WHEN Adam day by day
    Woke up in Paradise,
He always used to say,
    "Oh, this is very nice."

But Eve from scenes of bliss
    Transported him for life.
The more I think of this
    The more I beat my wife.

A. E. Housman

I Burned My Candle at Both Ends

I BURNED my candle at both ends,
And now have neither foes nor friends;
For all the lovely light begotten,
I'm paying now in feeling rotten.

Samuel Hoffenstein

A St. Cecilia's Day Epigram

ANNOTATORS agree Composer X
Though always in love never had sex,

While a thousand motets and masses lie
To the credit of sex-mad Composer Y,

And that lover of life, Composer Z,
In his operas wishes he were dead.

Each in his paradoxical way
Does a lot for the famous critic K.

Peter Porter

Overheard in the Louvre

SAID the Victory of Samothrace,
What winning's worth this loss of face?

X. J. Kennedy

THIS *Humanist* whom no beliefs constrained
Grew so broad-minded he was scatter-brained.

J. V. Cunningham

Temptation

TEMPTATION, temptation, temptation,
Dick Barton went down to the station,
Blondie was there
All naked and bare,
Temptation, temptation, temptation.

English children's street rhyme

On Mundane Acquaintances

GOOD morning, Algernon: Good morning, Percy.
Good morning, Mrs. Roebuck. Christ have mercy!

Hilaire Belloc

To a Man in a Picture Window Watching Television

WATCHING TV,
How aptly
You're framed,
As if on TV—
Observer observed!

Deeper in shade,
Still others may sit
Watching me
Watching you
Watching it.

Mildred Weston

John Wesley Gaines

JOHN Wesley Gaines!
John Wesley Gaines!
Thou monumental mass of brains!
Come in, John Wesley
For it rains.

Anonymous

(Clifton Fadiman notes in his *The American Treasury* that "Mr. Gaines is believed to have been a congressman.")

The Bookworms

THROUGH and through the inspirèd leaves,
    Ye maggots, make your windings;
But, oh! respect his lordship's taste,
    And spare his golden bindings!

Robert Burns

Race Prejudice

LITTLE mouse:
Are you
some rat's little child?
I won't love you if you are.

Alfred Kreymborg

The Van Gogh Influence

TELL me Beatrice
What would you do
If I cut off my ear for you
And to this letter I attached it?
—You'd write me back for the one that matched it.

Shel Silverstein

V

"Here dead lie we ..."

Here Dead Lie We Because We Did Not Choose

HERE dead lie we because we did not choose
    To live and shame the land from which we sprung.
Life, to be sure, is nothing much to lose;
    But young men think it is, and we were young.

A. E. Housman

Gaily I Lived

GAILY I lived as ease and nature taught,
And spent my little life without a thought;
And am annoyed that Death, that tyrant grim,
Should think of me, who never thought of him.

Anonymous
(seventeenth century)

On Middleton Edge

IF this life-saving rock should fail
Yielding too much to my embrace
And rock and I to death should race,
The rock would stay there in the dale
While I, breaking my fall,
Would still go on
Farther than any wandering star has gone.

Andrew Young

An Inscription by the Sea
(After a poem in the Greek Anthology)

No dust have I to cover me,
    My grave no man may show;
My tomb is this unending sea,
    And I lie far below.
My fate, O stranger, was to drown;
And where it was the ship went down
    Is what the sea-birds know.

Edward Arlington Robinson

Epitaph on Dr. Johnson

HERE lies Sam Johnson: Reader have a care,
Tread lightly, lest you wake a sleeping bear:
Religious, moral, generous, and humane
He was; but self-sufficient, proud, and vain,
Fond of, and overbearing in, dispute,
A Christian and a scholar—but a brute.

Soame Jenyns

To the Oaks of Glencree

MY arms are round you, and I lean
Against you, while the lark
Sings over us, and golden lights and green
Shadows are on your bark.

There'll come a season when you'll stretch
Black boards to cover me:
Then in Mount Jerome I will lie, poor wretch,
With worms eternally.

John Millington Synge

At My Father's Grave

THE sunlicht still on me, you row'd in clood,
We look upon each ither noo like hills
Across a valley. I'm nae mair your son.
In my mind, nae son o' yours, that looks,
And the great darkness o' your death comes up
And equals it across the way.
A livin' man upon a deid man thinks
And ony sma'er thocht's impossible.

Hugh MacDiarmid

---

row'd—rolled, wrapped up

The Husband

WHEN the man arrives tomorrow, bearing a token:
"Come, I will show you. Leave everything here;
dead weight; none of it matters," will I go?

A wife, two kids, my manuscripts, my car?
When I am eighty, and have outlived my debtors,
once more he will come. Then I'll go with him.

Donald Finkel

The Bustle in a House

THE bustle in a house
The morning after death
Is solemnest of industries
Enacted upon earth,—

The sweeping up the heart,
And putting love away
We shall not want to use again
Until eternity.

Emily Dickinson

Resurrection Song

THREAD the nerves through the right holes,
Get out of my bones, you wormy souls.
Shut up my stomach, the ribs are full:
Muscles be steady and ready to pull.
Heart and artery merrily shake
And eyelids go up, for we're ready to wake.—
His eye must be brighter—one more rub!
And pull up the nostrils! his nose was snub.

Thomas Lovell Beddoes

"I Am a Sioux Brave," He Said in Minneapolis

HE is just plain drunk.
He knows no more than I do
What true waters to mourn for,
Or what kind of words to sing
When he dies.

James Wright

Morality

OBSERVE the Roman Forum; turn away.
That pasture of cold time has had its day.
Smile as you say this who will be
Dust when these stones still mark the Sacred Way.

Jean Garrigue

Thaw

IN time the snowman always dies,
As even children realize,
And do not mourn his sad demise.
In April, when he's long been gone
And I begin to mow the lawn,
The blades will crack his big black eyes.

Walker Gibson

Heraclitus

THEY told me, Heraclitus, they told me you were dead,
They brought me bitter news to hear and bitter tears to shed.
I wept as I remembered how often you and I
Had tired the sun with talking and sent him down the sky.

And now that thou are lying, my dear old Carian guest,
A handful of grey ashes, long, long ago at rest,
Still are thy pleasant voices, thy nightingales, awake;
For Death, he taketh all away, but them he cannot take.

William Johnson Cory

Madrigal

YOUR love is dead, lady, your love is dead;
Dribbles no sound
From his stopped lips, though swift underground
Spurts his wild hair.

Your love is dead, lady, your love is dead;
Faithless he lies
Deaf to your call, though shades of his eyes
Break through and stare.

R. S. Thomas

Cremation

It nearly cancels my fear of death, my dearest said,
When I think of cremation. To rot in the earth
Is a loathsome end, but to roar up in flame—besides, I
    am used to it,
I have flamed with love or fury so often in my life,
No wonder my body is tired, no wonder it is dying,
We had great joy of my body. Scatter the ashes.

Robinson Jeffers

Ballad

Father, through the dark that parts us,
Through the howling winds I hear,
Come and drive away this dabbled
Ghost I fear.

*But I've crossed the dark already
And am part of all you hear,
I shall never leave you, darling,
Do not fear.*

Roy Fuller

A Recollection

MY father's friend came once to tea.
He laughed and talked. He spoke to me.
But in another week they said
That friendly pink-faced man was dead.

"How sad . . ." they said, "the best of men . . ."
So I said too, "How sad"; but then
Deep in my heart I thought, with pride,
"I know a person who has died."

Frances Cornford

Henry Turnbull

HE planked down sixpence and he took his drink;
Then slowly picked the change up from the zinc,
And in his breeches-pocket buttoned tight
Two greasy pennies, which that very night
Were used by Betty Catchieside, called in
To lay him out, when she'd tied up his chin,
To keep his eyelids shut: and so he lies
With tuppence change till Doomsday on his eyes.

Wilfrid Gibson

Anonymous Gravestone

ALTHOUGH his actions won him wide renown,
With praise we cannot be profuse,
And thus prefer to leave his name unknown.
Because for all the things he left undone
There is no possible excuse.

> *Erich Kästner*
> *Translated from the German*
> *by Patrick Bridgewater*

"Bona de Mortuis"

AY, ay; *good man, kind father, best of friends*—
These are the words that grow, like grass and nettles,
Out of dead men, and speckled hatreds hide,
Like toads, among them.

> *Thomas Lovell Beddoes*

In the Museum

SMALL and emptied woman you lie here a thousand years dead
your hands on your diminished loins flat in this final bed
teeth jutting from your unwound head your spiced bones black
      and dried,
who knew you and kissed you and kept you and wept when you
      died;
died you young had you grace? Risus sardonicus replied.
Then quick I seized my husband's hand while he stared at his
      bride.

Isabella Gardner

Little Elegy
for a child who skipped rope

HERE lies resting, out of breath,
Out of turns, Elizabeth
Whose quicksilver toes not quite
Cleared the whirring edge of night.

Earth whose circles round us skim
Till they catch the lightest limb,
Shelter now Elizabeth
And for her sake trip up Death.

X. J. Kennedy

An Old Atheist Pauses by the Sea

I CHOOSE at random, knowing less and less.
The shambles of the seashore at my feet
Yield a weathered spiral: I confess
—Appalled at how the waves have polished it—
I know that shores are eaten, rocks are split,
Shells ghosted. Something hates unevenness.
The skin turns porcelain, the nerves retreat,
And then the will, and then the consciousness.

Thomas Kinsella

Epitaph of a Faithful Man

YOU of the covered breasts, the lovely head,
Must now be withered, or like me, a ghost—
Say that some women had of me a token
Of that long love which you alone could boast;
Say that I slept in many another's bed—
I sleep here now, my oath still unbroken.

Robert Mezey

On a Row of Nuns in a Cemetery

EACH, the issue of a passioned kiss,
Renounced her birthright for superior bliss;
Attaining, lastly, this.

R. G. Howarth

Slim Cunning Hands

SLIM cunning hands at rest, and cozening eyes—
Under this stone one loved too wildly lies;
How false she was, no granite could declare;
  Nor all earth's flowers, how fair.

Walter de la Mare

MUST
All this aching
Go to making
Dust?

Alun Lewis

Epitaph

WHEN I shall be without regret
And shall mortality forget,
When I shall die who lived for this,
I shall not miss the things I miss.
And you who notice where I lie
Ask not my name. It is not I.

J. V. Cunningham

Lying in State

HE'S dead. Into the vault and out
Shuffles the reverent conga.
With his intestines taken out.
He will stay sweeter longer.

Adrian Mitchell

The Death of the Ball Turret Gunner

FROM my mother's sleep I fell into the State,
And I hunched in its belly till my wet fur froze.
Six miles from earth, loosed from its dream of life,
I woke to black flak and the nightmare fighters.
When I died they washed me out of the turret with a hose.

Randall Jarrell

War Story

OF one who grew up at Gallipoli
Not over months and miles, but in the space
Of feet and half a minute. Wading shoreward
With a plague of bullets pocking the sea
He tripped, as it seemed to him over his scabbard,
And stubbed his fingers on a dead man's face.

Jon Stallworthy

The General

"GOOD morning; good morning!" the General said
When we met him last week on our way to the line.
Now the soldiers he smiled at are most of 'em dead,
And we're cursing his staff for incompetent swine.
"He's a cheery old card," grunted Harry to Jack
As they slogged up to Arras with rifle and pack.

* * * *

But he did for them both with his plan of attack.

Siegfried Sassoon

Fragment

BURY him deep. So damned a work should lie
Nearer the Devil than man. Make him a bed
Beneath some lock-jawed hell, that never yawns
With earthquake or eruption; and so deep
That he may hear the devil and his wife
In bed, talking secrets.

Thomas Lovell Beddoes

A Question

I ASKED if I got sick and died, would you
With my black funeral go walking too
If you'd stand close to hear them talk or pray
While I'm let down in that steep bank of clay.
And, No, you said, for if you saw a crew
Of living idiots, pressing round that new
Oak coffin—they alive, I dead beneath
That board—you'd rave and rend them with your teeth.

John Millington Synge

Presentiment Is That Long Shadow on the Lawn

PRESENTIMENT is that long shadow on the lawn
Indicative that suns go down;
The notice to the startled grass
That darkness is about to pass.

Emily Dickinson

Epitaph for a Timid Lady

WHEN I was born a happy child
The waves ahead looked sweet and wild.
I lie beneath this final sheet
Who never found them wild or sweet.
I did not wish to wet my feet.

Frances Cornford

Ah! Sun-Flower

AH, Sun-flower! weary of time
Who countest the steps of the Sun;
Seeking after that sweet golden clime,
Where the traveller's journey is done;

Where the Youth pined away with desire,
And the pale Virgin shrouded in snow,
Arise from their graves, and aspire
Where my Sun-flower wishes to go.

William Blake

VI

"It rests me to be among beautiful women ..."

Tame Cat

"It rests me to be among beautiful women.
Why should one always lie about such matters?
I repeat:
It rests me to converse with beautiful women
Even though we talk nothing but nonsense,

The purring of the invisible antennae
Is both stimulating and delightful."

Ezra Pound

How Music's Made

Study this violent and trembling woman
who is a gut strung from star to star
and when she's struck must twang till all the cups
and saucers ring and shake upon their shelves.
Forehear the note. Be thoughtful where you pluck.
How music's made is not a thing of luck.

Dilys Laing

Birch

BIRCH tree, you remind me
Of a room filled with breathing,
The sway and whisper of love.

She slips off her shoes;
Unzips her skirt; arms raised,
Unclasps an earring, and the other.

Just so the sallow trunk
Divides, and the branches
Are pale and smooth.

Louis Simpson

A Bed Without a Woman

A BED without a woman
Is a thing of wood and springs, a pit
To roll in with the Devil. But let
Her body touch its length and it becomes
A place of singing wonders, eager springboard
To heaven and higher. And you may join her there
In those hours between sleeping and dawn.

Raymond Souster

Great Man

WHAT was it like to
live then? we asked him,
who had lived through it.

Bad, he said, it was
not good. I envy
you missing it all.

He seemed bored by our
questions, interested
more in our women.

B. S. Johnson

Women

GIVE me a Girlie (if one I needs must meet)
Or in her Nuptiall, or her winding sheet;
I know but two good Houres that women have,
One in the Bed, another in the Grave.
Thus of the whole Sex all I would desire,
Is to enjoy their Ashes, or their Fire.

William Cartwright

In the Dark None Dainty

NIGHT hides our thefts; all faults then pardoned be:
All are alike fair when no spots we see.
Lais and Lucretia in the night-time are
Pleasing alike; alike both singular:
Joan and my lady have at that time one
One and the self-same prized complexion.
Then please alike the pewter and the plate,
The chosen ruby and the reprobate.

Robert Herrick

The Beautiful

THREE things there are more beautiful
    Than any man could wish to see:
The first, it is a full-rigged ship
    Sailing with all her sails set free;
The second, when the wind and sun
    Are playing in a field of corn;
The third, a woman, young and fair,
    Showing her child before it is born.

W. H. Davies

The Yawn

THE black-haired girl
With the big
                    brown
                              eyes
on the Queens train coming
                    in to work, so
opens her mouth so beautifully
                    wide
                              in a ya-aawn, that
two stops after she has left the train
I have only to think of her and i
                                        o-oh-aaaww-hm
                                        wow !

Paul Blackburn

Juliet

How did the party go in Portman Square?
I cannot tell you; Juliet was not there.
And how did Lady Gaster's party go?
Juliet was next me and I do not know.

Hilaire Belloc

"It rests me to be among beautiful women . . ."   93

Summum Bonum

ALL the breath and the bloom of the year in the
    bag of one bee:
All the wonder and wealth of the mine in the
    heart of one gem:
In the core of one pearl all the shade and the
    shine of the sea:
Breath and bloom, shade and shine, wonder,
    wealth, and how far above them—
    Truth, that's brighter than gem,
    Trust, that's purer than pearl,
Brightest truth, purest trust in the universe
    In the kiss of one girl.

Robert Browning

Green

THE dawn was apple-green,
The sky was green wine held up in the sun,
The moon was a gold petal between.

She opened her eyes, and green
They shone, clear like flowers undone
For the first time, now for the first time seen.

D. H. Lawrence

Inconsistent

LET no man see my girl;
Let all see, and admire.
Why do I contradict
Myself? Do not inquire.

Mark Van Doren

Spectrum

BROWN from the sun's mid-afternoon caress,
And where not brown, white as a bridal dress,
And where not white, pink as an opened plum.

And where not pink, darkly mysterious,
And when observed, openly furious,
And then obscured, while the red blushes come.

William Dickey

VII

"… into the daily accident."

Morning Song

Look, it's morning, and a little water gurgles in the tap.
I wake up waiting, because it's Sunday, and turn twice more
than usual in the bed, before I rise to cereal and comic strips.
I have risen to the morning danger and feel proud,
and after shaving off the night's disguises, after searching
close to the bone for blood, and finding only a little,
I shall walk out bravely into the daily accident.

Alan Dugan

I Wonder How Many People in This City

I wonder how many people in this city
live in furnished rooms.
Late at night when I look out at the buildings
I swear I see a face in every window
looking back at me,
and when I turn away
I wonder how many go back to their desks
and write this down.

Leonard Cohen

Reflections in a Little Park

On dusty benches in the park
I see them sit from noon till dark,
Infirm and dull, or glum and dry,
And think, as I go stepping by:
"There—but for the Grace of God—sit I!"
Yet cannot blink and cannot bless
God's manifest ungraciousness.

Babette Deutsch

To a Fat Lady Seen from the Train

O why do you walk through the fields in gloves,
    Missing so much and so much?
O fat white woman whom nobody loves,
Why do you walk through the fields in gloves,
When the grass is soft as the breast of doves
    And shivering sweet to the touch?
O why do you walk through the fields in gloves
    Missing so much and so much?

Frances Cornford

Between the Acts

FATE hired me once to play a villain's part.
I did it badly, wasting valued blood;
Now when the call is given to the good,
It is that knave who answers in my heart.

Stanley Kunitz

Junker Schmidt

THE leaf is wilting. Summer drains out.
    Now the frost lies silver.
Junker Schmidt, from a revolver,
    Wants to blow his brains out.

But wait, you madman, wait! Learn:
    Greenery shall live on.
Junker Schmidt, my word of honor,
    Summer will return.

"Kozma Prutkov"
Translated by W. D. Snodgrass
and Tanya Tolstoy

"Kozma Prutkov" is a hoax poet invented by Count Alexi Tolstoy and his friends.

This World and This Life Are So Scattered, They Try Me

THIS world and this life are so scattered, they try me,
And so to a German professor I'll hie me.
He can well put all the fragments together
Into a system convenient and terse;
While with his night-cap and dressing-robe tatters
He'll stop up the chink of the wide Universe.

Heinrich Heine
Translated by Charles Godfrey Leland

Memorandum for Minos

INFLATED boys, when clergymen are odd,
Compress with handkerchiefs their bulging laughter.

(As children in the bathroom torture taps,
Stubbing explosive water with their thumbs.)

So congregations chained in sulphurous pews
Might gag their giggling through an endless sermon.

Richard Kell

All the Smoke

ALL the smoke
Rising
From McKeesport, Pa.,
On an afternoon
In twilight,
Weighs
Two pounds, net.

Eli Siegel

DR. Hu
speaks
twenty-three
    languages.

What loneliness.

Norman Mailer

I May, I Might, I Must

IF you will tell me why the fen
appears impassable, I then
Will tell you why I think that I
can get across it if I try.

Marianne Moore

". . . into the daily accident." 103

Political Reflection

loquitur the sparrow in the zoo

No bars are set too close, no mesh too fine
To keep me from the eagle and the lion,
Whom keepers feed that I may freely dine.
This goes to show that if you have the wit
To be small, common, cute, and live on shit,
Though the cage fret kings, you may make free with it.

Howard Nemerov

The Wheel Change

I'M sitting on the grass by the roadside.
The driver is changing the wheel.
I don't like it where I come from.
I don't like it where I'm going to.
Why am I watching the wheel change
With impatience?

Bertolt Brecht
Translated from the German
by Eric Bentley

Open to Visitors

A NOBLE hedge of ancient yew
Conceals the house from public view;
Within the house a private room
Conceals a public man of whom
The public image, distant, cold,
Conceals, they say, a heart of gold;
But what the heart of gold conceals
No one, no one at all, reveals.

E. V. Milner

Trying to Sleep

THERE is dark.
I can't hold it.
Dogs bark
down in the street.

I've shut the blind
but repeat
the cut of the moon
in my mind.

Ralph Pomeroy

". . . into the daily accident." 105

In the Suburbs

THERE's no way out.
You were born to waste your life.
You were born to this middleclass life

As others before you
Were born to walk in the procession
To the temple, singing.

Louis Simpson

Picture Framing

MY fingers feed in the fields of wood.

I sand pine, walnut, oak,
and sweat to raise their grain.

Paints, powder and brush
are the seasons of my trade.

And at the end of day
I drive home
the proud cattle of my hands.

Bert Meyers

The Young Recruit

IN these firm ranks a load slips from his soul.
The daily strife for petty gains can cease.
At last a comrade in some larger whole,
He has escaped the private wars of peace.

Arthur Davison Ficke

Faith Is a Fine Invention

FAITH is a fine invention
For gentlemen who see;
But microscopes are prudent
In an emergency!

Emily Dickinson

Vice

VICE is a monster of so frightful mien,
As to be hated, needs but to be seen;
Yet seen too oft, familiar with her face,
We first endure, then pity, then embrace.

Alexander Pope

"... into the daily accident."

Nescit vox missa reverti . . .

THE once hooked ever after lives in lack,
And the once said never finds its way back.

J. V. Cunningham

God and Man

AFTER casting the first act, checking sections
of scenery and mastering his rage
because the female lead blundered on page
one, he left the actors to themselves on stage
without a script and fretting for directions.

Samuel Hazo

The Halt

THE halt looks into the eyes of the halt and looks away.
No response there that he can see
To receive amply or repay.

But the halt will lead the blind; indeed
Note how the generous stick gestures to precede
The blind, blundering in his black, black, black need.

Josephine Miles

Gasco, or The Toad

In back of our town
there's a toad who squats on
    the gasworks
when he breathes in and out
    we can cook

Günter Grass
Translated from the German
by Jerome Rothenberg

In a Parlor Containing a Table

In a parlor containing a table
And three chairs, three men confided
Their inmost thoughts to one another.
I, said the first, am miserable.
I am miserable, the second said.
I think that for me the correct word
Is miserable, asserted the third.
Well, they said at last, it's quarter to two.
Good night. Cheer up. Sleep well.
You too. You too. You too.

Galway Kinnell

". . . into the daily accident."

Outwitted

HE drew a circle that shut me out—
Heretic, rebel, a thing to flout.
But Love and I had the wit to win:
We drew a circle that took him in!

Edwin Markham

Time Piece

TAKE the back off the watch
and see that universe of small parts,
bobbing and turning,
each doing what it should be doing,
and ignoring you completely.

William Cole

Bear in Mind, O Ye Recording Angels

BEAR in mind, o ye recording angels,
That all of us, from the Pope to Stalin,
From Lavatory Dan to John D. Rockefeller,
Are children gazing in a sweetshop window.

Norman Cameron

VIII

"Nature, like us, is sometimes caught
Without her diadem."

The Sky Is Low, the Clouds Are Mean

THE sky is low, the clouds are mean,
A traveling flake of snow
Across a barn or through a rut
Debates if it will go.

A narrow wind complains all day
How some one treated him;
Nature, like us, is sometimes caught
Without her diadem.

Emily Dickinson

Exeunt

PIECEMEAL the summer dies;
At the field's edge a daisy lives alone;
A last shawl of burning lies
On a gray field-stone.

All cries are thin and terse;
The field has droned the summer's final mass;
A cricket like a dwindled hearse
Crawls from the dry grass.

Richard Wilbur

"Nature . . . caught without her diadem."

Spring Oak

ABOVE the quiet valley and unrippled lake
While woodchucks burrowed new holes, and birds sang,
And radicles began downward and shoots
Committed themselves to the spring
And entered with tiny industrious earthquakes,
A dry-rooted, winter-twisted oak
Revealed itself slowly. And one morning
When the valley underneath was still sleeping
It shook itself and was all green.

Galway Kinnell

Tall Nettles

TALL nettles cover up, as they have done
These many springs, the rusty harrow, the plough
Long worn out, and the roller made of stone:
Only the elm butt tops the nettles now.

This corner of the farmyard I like most:
As well as any bloom upon a flower
I like the dust on the nettles, never lost
Except to prove the sweetness of a shower.

Edward Thomas

One A. M.

THE storm came home too blind to stand:
He thwacked down oaks like chairs
And missing foothold in the dark
Rolled ominous downstairs,

And fumbling with a giant hand
Made nine white tries to scratch
Against a shuddering wall of air
The strict head of his match.

X. J. Kennedy

After the Party

BANISH the scent of sherry and cigars,
Throw back the shutters, quench the cultured light,
Let in the air. O fresher than the stars
The rank, primeval innocent smell of night!

Frances Cornford

"Nature . . . caught without her diadem."

Snow

How can snow sifting so fine
You look sharp to see a flake
Fill a mile of air like smoke
And hide Great Oak Hill from sight?

John Kelleher

Winter Ocean

MANY-MANED scud-thumper, tub
of male whales, maker of worn wood, shrub-
ruster, sky-mocker, rave!
portly pusher of waves, wind-slave.

John Updike

Thaw

OVER the land freckled with snow half-thawed
The speculating rooks at their nests cawed
And saw from elm-tops, delicate as flower of grass,
What we below could not see, Winter pass.

Edward Thomas

The Wind

THE wind stood up, and gave a shout;
He whistled on his fingers, and

Kicked the withered leaves about,
And thumped the branches with his hand,

And said he'd kill, and kill, and kill;
And so he will! And so he will!

James Stephens

What's the Railroad to Me?

WHAT'S the railroad to me?
I never go to see
Where it ends.
It fills a few hollows,
And makes banks for the swallows,
It sets the sand a-blowing,
And the blackberries a-growing.

Henry David Thoreau

The Routine

EACH day I open the cupboard
& the green shoots of my last onion
have in the dark grown higher

A perverse & fairly final pleasure
That I love to watch him stretching himself
secretly, green sprouting shamelessly in
this winter, making a park in my kitchen, making
spring for a moment in my kitchen

that, instead of eating him
I have watched him grow

Paul Blackburn

Walnut

WALNUT: compressed wisdom,
Tiny vegetable turtle,
Brain of an elf
Paralyzed for eternity.

Jorge Carrera Andrade
Translated from the Spanish
by Philip Silver

IX

"As I was old sometime and sometime young ..."

Time's Mutability

(1)

As I was old sometime and sometime young
Old in the morning, young again at dusk
And was a child, remembering great grief
And was an old man void of memory.

(2)

I was sad when I was young
And am sad now I am old
So when can I be gay for once?
It had better be soon.

Bertolt Brecht
Translated from the German
by Martin Esslin

Autumn

HE told his life story to Mrs. Courtly
Who was a widow. "Let us get married shortly,"
He said. "I am no longer passionate,
But we can have some conversation before it is too late."

Stevie Smith

The Act

THERE were the roses, in the rain.
Don't cut them, I pleaded.
        They won't last, she said
But they're so beautiful
      where they are.
Agh, we were all beautiful once, she
      said,
and cut them and gave them to me
      in my hand.

William Carlos Williams

After Long Silence

SPEECH after long silence; it is right,
All other lovers being estranged or dead,
Unfriendly lamplight hid under its shade,
The curtains drawn upon unfriendly night,
That we descant and yet again descant
Upon the supreme theme of Art and Song:
Bodily decrepitude is wisdom; young
We loved each other and were ignorant.

W. B. Yeats

Age

DEATH, tho I see him not, is near
And grudges me my eightieth year.
Now, I would give him all these last
For one that fifty have run past.
Ah! he strikes all things, all alike,
But bargains: those he will not strike.

Walter Savage Landor

The Embankment

(The fantasia of a fallen gentleman on a cold, bitter night)

ONCE, in a finesse of fiddles found I ecstasy,
In a flash of gold heels on the hard pavement.
Now see I
That warmth's the very stuff of poesy.
Oh, God, make small
The old star-eaten blanket of the sky,
That I may fold it round me and in comfort lie.

T. E. Hulme

In the Tub We Soak Our Skin

IN the tub we soak our skin
And drowse and meditate within.

The mirror clouds, the vapors rise,
We view our toes with sad surprise:

The toes that mother kissed and counted,
The since neglected and unwanted.

Edward Newman Horn

As Bad as a Mile

WATCHING the shied core
Striking the basket, skidding across the floor,
Shows less and less of luck, and more and more

Of failure spreading back up the arm
Earlier and earlier, the unraised hand calm,
The apple unbitten in the palm.

Philip Larkin

The Summing-Up

WHEN I was young I scribbled, boasting, on my wall,
No Love, No Property, No Wages.
In youth's good time I somehow bought them all,
And cheap, you'd think, for maybe a hundred pages.

Now in my prime, disburdened of my gear,
My trophies ransomed, broken, lost,
I carve again on the lintel of the year
My sign: *Mobility*—and damn the cost!

Stanley Kunitz

Old Dan'l

OUT of his cottage to the sun
Bent double comes old Dan'l,
His chest all over cotton wool,
His back all over flannel.

"Winter will finish him," they've said
Each winter now for ten:
But comes the first warm day of Spring
Old Dan'l's out again.

L. A. G. Strong

"As I was old sometime and sometime young . . ."

Advice to Young Children

"CHILDREN who paddle where the ocean bed shelves steeply
Must take great care they do not,
Paddle too deeply."

Thus spake the awful aging couple
Whose heart the years had turned to rubble.

But the little children, to save any bother,
Let it in at one ear and out at the other.

Stevie Smith

The Flesh-Scraper

IF I had sight enough
Might I not find a finger-print
Left on this flint
By Neolithic man or Kelt?
So knapped to scrape a wild beast's pelt,
The thumb below, fingers above,
See, my hand fits it like a glove.

Andrew Young

Long Distance

SOMETIMES when you watch the fire
ashes glow and gray
the way the sun turned cold on spires
in winter in the town back home
so far away.

Sometimes on the telephone
the one you hear goes far
and ghostly voices whisper in.
You think they are from other wires.
You think they are.

William Stafford

Absent-minded Professor

THIS lonely figure of not much fun
Strayed out of folklore fifteen years ago
Forever. Now on an autumn afternoon,
While the leaves drift past the office window,
His bright replacement, present-minded, stays
At the desk correcting papers, nor ever grieves
For the silly scholar of the bad old days,
Who'd burn the papers and correct the leaves.

Howard Nemerov

Youth

A YOUNG Apollo, golden-haired,
    Stands dreaming on the verge of strife,
Magnificently unprepared
    For the long littleness of life.

Frances Cornford

Difficult Times

STANDING at my writing desk
I see through the window in the garden the
       elder bush
And in it vaguely discern some red and black
And suddenly I remember the elder bush
Of my childhood in Augsburg.
And for several minutes I
Seriously consider whether I should
Go to the table to get my glasses, to see
The black berries again on their red twigs.

Bertolt Brecht
Translated from the German
by Martin Esslin

I Was Born upon Thy Bank, River

I WAS born upon thy bank, river,
    My blood flows in thy stream,
And thou meanderest forever
    At the bottom of my dream.

Henry David Thoreau

Another Return

WHY, when we were dressed for darker weather,
Did you walk in that slim green gown
That bared your shoulders and almost your breasts
And the young hair that way down to your shoulders?
As though you were quoting light.

Lie down. Lie down again beside me.
Was your reluctance for the others there?
Or, because you had not changed as I,
You had forgotten me and all those times?
Lie down again beside me.

Winfield Townley Scott

"As I was old sometime and sometime young . . ."   *129*

The Witch

TOIL and grow rich,
What's that but to lie
With a foul witch
And after, drained dry,
To be brought
To the chamber where
Lies one long sought
With despair?

W. B. Yeats

When I Peruse the Conquer'd Fame

WHEN I peruse the conquer'd fame of heroes and the victories
    of mighty generals, I do not envy the generals,
Nor the President in his Presidency, nor the rich in his great
    house,
But when I hear of the brotherhood of lovers, how it was
    with them,
How together through life, through dangers, odium, unchang-
    ing, long and long,
Through youth and middle age and old age, how unfaltering,
    how affectionate and faithful they were,
Then I am pensive—I hastily walk away fill'd with the bitterest
    envy.

Walt Whitman

The Single Woman

Now quenched each midnight window is. Now un-
        impeded
Darkness indeed descends on roof and tree and slope;
And in my heart the houses that you have not needed
Put out their coloured lights of comfort and of hope.

Frances Cornford

Pad, Pad

I ALWAYS remember your beautiful flowers
And the beautiful kimono you wore
When you sat on the couch
With that tigerish crouch
And told me you loved me no more.

What I cannot remember is how I felt when you were unkind
All I know is, if you were unkind now I should not mind.
Ah me, the power to feel exaggerated, angry and sad
The years have taken from me. Softly I go now, pad pad.

Stevie Smith

X

"... by the world oppressed"

Youth and Age

MUCH did I rage when young,
Being by the world oppressed,
But now with flattering tongue
It speeds the parting guest.

W. B. Yeats

Gift to a Jade

FOR love he offered me his perfect world.
This world was so constricted, and so small,
It had no sort of loveliness at all,
And I flung back the little silly ball.
At that cold moralist I hotly hurled
His perfect, pure, symmetrical, small world.

Anna Wickham

Waking

I SAID to myself one morning:
    "Annie, the world is fair;
You'd better be up and combing
    The tangles out of your hair."

Quickly myself made answer:
    "The world is horrid and queer,
And if you don't go to sleep again
    You're going to be sorry, dear."

Annie Higgins

The Leaden-Eyed

LET not young souls be smothered out before
They do quaint deeds and fully flaunt their pride.
It is the world's one crime its babes grow dull,
Its poor are ox-like, limp and leaden-eyed.
Not that they starve, but starve so dreamlessly;
Not that they sow, but that they seldom reap;
Not that they serve, but have no gods to serve;
Not that they die, but that they die like sheep.

Vachel Lindsay

Search

Not another bite, not another cigarette,
Nor a final coffee from the shining coffee-urn before you leave
The warmth steaming at the windows of the hamburger-joint
          where the Wurlitzer
Booms all night without a stop, where the onions are thick
          between the buns.
Wrap yourself well in that cheap coat that holds back the
          wind like a sieve,
You have a long way to go, and the streets are dark, you may
          have to walk all night before you find
Another heart as lonely, so nearly mad with boredom, so filled
          with such strength, such tenderness of love.

Raymond Souster

Parable

All night the men whipped the dead horse and then
When morning broke they rose up and whipped it again
Until their arms fell to their sides heavy as lead,
But the horse remained dead.

Meanwhile their sons, growing bored,
Attacked each other with knives
And ganged up to rape those lonely women,
Their fathers' mothers, daughters, and wives.

Peggy Bennett

Eagle Valor, Chicken Mind

UNHAPPY country, what wings you have! Even here,
Nothing important to protect, and ocean-far from the nearest
      enemy, what a cloud
Of bombers amazes the coast mountain, what a hornet-swarm
      of fighters,
And day and night the guns practicing.

Unhappy, eagle wings and beak, chicken brain.
Weep (it is frequent in human affairs), weep for the terrible
      magnificence of the means,
The ridiculous incompetence of the reasons, the bloody and
      shabby
Pathos of the result.

Robinson Jeffers

Four Lovely Sisters

FOUR lovely spinsters, sisters to a king
Thrown in a monastery asked for one thing,
And it was granted: Permission to eat
Elaborate dishes of fish and of meat.
It was good—so the Christian chronicle runs—
For the round-eyed other nuns,
Who fasted and were not exempted,
To watch their Highnesses without being tempted.

C. A. Trypanis

Take One Home for the Kiddies

On shallow straw, in shadeless glass,
Huddled by empty bowls, they sleep:
No dark, no dam, no earth, no grass—
Mam, get us one of them to keep.

Living toys are something novel,
But it soon wears off somehow.
Fetch the shoebox, fetch the shovel—
Mam, we're playing funerals now.

Philip Larkin

My heart moves as heavy as the horse that climbs the hill,
And I can't for my dear life pretend to be happy.
You know nothing of the place on which my shoe is pinching,
And many, many troubled thoughts are quite breaking my
     heart.

Welsh folk poem
Translated by Menna Gallie

To the Wind at Morn

Is it for you
    The Larks sing loud,
The Leaves clap hands,
    The Lilies nod?
Do they forget
    The screams so wild,
Heard all the night—
    Where is that child?

W. H. Davies

Song for Mother's Day

AFTER twenty years of expensive foods
She sent her son back to the children-factory,
A label on his neck "Unsatisfactory."
But he came home again, with "Damaged Goods."

T. S. Matthews

All, All of a Piece

ALL, all of a piece throughout;
Thy chase had a beast in view,
Thy wars brought nothing about,
Thy lovers were all untrue;
'Tis well an old age is out
And time to begin a new.

John Dryden

Most Souls, 'Tis True, but Peep Out Once an Age

MOST souls, 'tis true, but peep out once an age,
Dull sullen pris'ners in the body's cage:
Dim lights of life, that burn a length of years
Useless, unseen, as lamps in sepulchres:
Like Eastern Kings a lazy state they keep,
And, close confin'd to their own palace, sleep.

Alexander Pope

Marian at the Pentecostal Meeting

MARIAN I cannot begrudge
　　the carnival of God,
the cotton candy of her faith
　　spun on a silver rod

to lick in bed; a timid girl,
　　neither admired nor clever,
Christ pity her and let her ride
　　God's carousel forever.

Alden A. Knowlan

Xmas Time

A LITTLE lonely girl
Went calmly off to bed
And all the Xmas that she had
Was in her little head.

Walta Karsner
(Written age nine)

from *Thirty Bob a Week*

I STEP into my heart and there I meet
    A god-almighty devil singing small,
Who would like to shout and whistle in the street,
    And squelch the passers flat against the wall;
If the whole world was a cake he had the power to take,
    He would take it, ask for more, and eat it all.

John Davidson

Much Madness Is Divinest Sense

MUCH madness is divinest sense
To a discerning eye;
Much sense the starkest madness.
'Tis the majority
In this, as all, prevails.
Assent, and you are sane;
Demur,—You're straightway dangerous,
And handled with a chain.

Emily Dickinson

The Stars Have Not Dealt Me the Worst They Could Do

THE stars have not dealt me the worst they could do:
My pleasures are plenty, my troubles are two.
But oh, my two troubles they reave me of rest,
The brains in my head and the heart in my breast.

Oh, grant me the ease that is granted so free,
The birthright of multitudes, give it to me,
That relish their victuals and rest on their bed
With flint in the bosom and guts in the head.

A. E. Housman

Une Vie

BUT when Grandpa, the miner, came back from the States
spouting tales wild and woolly, his teeth
slanting backwards, his pockets empty
and said Now darling, how about building that house
Grandma picked up her scissors and struck him through the
        heart

Pentti Saarikoski
Translated from the Finnish
by Anselm Hollo

Epitaph on a Tyrant

PERFECTION, of a kind, was what he was after,
And the poetry he invented was easy to understand;
He knew human folly like the back of his hand,
And was greatly interested in armies and fleets;
When he laughed, respectable senators burst with laughter,
And when he cried the little children died in the streets.

W. H. Auden

Dramatic Fragment

SIR, say no more.
Within me 'tis as if
The green and climbing eyesight of a cat
Crawled near my mind's poor birds.

Trumbull Stickney

Living in Sin

THE hasty sin of the young after a dance,
Awkward in clothes against a wall or crick-necked
In car, gives many a nun her tidy bed,
Full board and launderette. God-fearing State
Provides three pounds a week, our conscience money,
For every infant severed from the breast.

Austin Clarke

Shut Up, I Said

"SHUT up," I said. "You make me ill.
Be quiet. Begone. Bedamned. Be still!
You are a hiccuping of my brain,
A tic twitching the eyelid of my soul,

And I have had my fill of you.
Foresee. Forsake. Farewell.
Or prepare for a hot but interesting tour
Through a tight personal corner of hell."

Peggy Bennett

News of the Phoenix

THEY say the Phoenix is dying, some say dead.
Dead without issue is what one message said,
But that has been supressed, officially denied.
I think myself the man who sent it lied.
In any case, I'm told, he has been shot
As a precautionary measure, whether he did or not.

A. J. M. Smith

Discord in Childhood

OUTSIDE the house an ash-tree hung its terrible whips,
And at night when the wind rose, the lash of the tree
Shrieked and slashed the wind, as a ship's
Weird rigging in a storm shrieks hideously.

Within the house two voices arose, a slender lash
Whistling she-delirious rage, and the dreadful sound
Of a male thong booming and bruising, until it had drowned
The other voice in a silence of blood, 'neath the noise of
the ash.

D. H. Lawrence

Family Matters

In our museum—we always go there on Sundays—
they have opened a new department.
Our aborted children, pale, serious embryos,
sit there in plain glass jars
and worry about their parents' future.

Günter Grass
Translated from the German
by Michael Hamburger

The Magi

Now as at all times I can see in the mind's eye,
In their stiff, painted clothes, the pale unsatisfied ones
Appear and disappear in the blue depth of the sky
With all their ancient faces like rain-beaten stones,
And all their helms of silver hovering side by side,
And all their eyes still fixed, hoping to find once more,
Being by Calvary's turbulence unsatisfied,
The uncontrollable mystery on the bestial floor.

W. B. Yeats

XI

"Shake off your heavy trance
And leap into a dance ..."

Shake Off Your Heavy Trance

SHAKE off your heavy trance
    And leap into a dance
Such as no mortals use to tread;
    Fit only for Apollo
To play to for the moon to lead
    And all the stars to follow.

Francis Beaumont

Washed in Silver

GLEAMING in silver are the hills!
Blazing in silver is the sea!

And a silvery radiance spills
Where the moon drives royally!

Clad in silver tissue, I
March magnificently by!

James Stephens

There'd Be an Orchestra
from "Thousand-and-First Ship"

THERE'D be an orchestra
  Bingo! Bango!
Playing for us
  To dance the tango,
And people would clap
  When we arose
At her sweet face
  And my new clothes.

     F. Scott Fitzgerald

Is It the Morning? Is It the Little Morning?

Is it the morning? Is it the little morning
Just before dawn? How big the sun is!
Are those the birds? Their voices begin
Everywhere, whistling, piercing, and joyous
All over and in the air, speaking the words
Which are more than words, with mounting consciousness:
And everything begins to rise to the brightening
Of the slow light that ascends to the blaze's lightning!

     Delmore Schwartz

Vernal Sentiment

THOUGH the crocuses poke up their heads in the usual places,
The frog scum appear on the pond with the same froth of green,
And the boys moon at girls with last year's fatuous faces,
I never am bored, however familiar the scene.

When from under the barn the cat brings a similar litter,—
Two yellow and black, and one that looks in between,—
Though it all happened before, I cannot grow bitter:
I rejoice in the spring, as though no spring ever had been.

Theodore Roethke

Two Hundred Girls in Tights & Halters

Two Hundred Girls in tights & halters
Cowboyboots cutaway at the calves
White plumes jiggling from their helmets
Make Main Street swagger in a dream

Four Hundred Bluebreasts bound in bronze
Bodies follow a twirling stave of steel
In unison "Beethoven's Moonlight Sonata" playing
Each on her shining glockenspiel.

Daniel Hoffman

". . . leap into a dance . . ."   *153*

Duke of Parma's Ear

SOMETIME, I feel, I'll hear
Palestrina play, as he played
When the Duke of Parma asked
Him to play:
For the Duke of Parma's ear.

Eli Siegel

The Bottle of Chianti

WHEN I pulled the cork
from the bottle of Chianti
I threw away the undergarment
of straw wrapped around it.

So it stands now in the cold tomb
of the refrigerator
quite naked
unashamed
shivering deliciously

Raymond Souster

Epitaph from The Great Gatsby

THEN wear the gold hat, if that will move her;
  If you can bounce high, bounce for her too.
Till she cry "Lover, gold-hatted, high-bouncing lover,
  I must have you!"

Thomas Parke D'Invilliers
(F. Scott Fitzgerald)

Explanation, on Coming Home Late

  WE went down to the river's brink
  To of those clear waters drink,
  Where the fishes, gold and red,
  Ever quickly past us sped,

  And the pebbles, red and blue,
  Which we saw the green weeds through
  At the bottom shining lay:
  It was their shining made us stay.

Richard Hughes
(Written age seven)

Temperament

In all thy humors, whether grave or mellow,
Thou'rt such a touchy, testy, pleasant fellow,
Hast so much wit and mirth and spleen about thee,
There is no living with thee nor without thee.

Martial
Translated by Joseph Addison

Driving to Town Late to Mail a Letter

It is a cold and snowy night. The main street is deserted.
The only things moving are swirls of snow.
As I lift the mailbox door, I feel its cold iron.
There is a privacy I love in this snowy night.
Driving around, I will waste more time.

Robert Bly

The Coming of Good Luck

So good luck came, and on my roof did light
Like noiseless snow, or as the dew of night:
Not all at once, but gently, as the trees
Are by the sunbeams tickled by degrees.

Robert Herrick

Child on Top of a Greenhouse

THE wind billowing out the seat of my britches,
My feet crackling splinters of glass and dried putty,
The half-grown chrysanthemums staring up like accusers,
Up through the streaked glass, flashing with sunlight,
A few white clouds all rushing eastward,
A line of elms plunging and tossing like horses,
And everyone, everyone pointing up and shouting!

Theodore Roethke

The Crackling Twig

THERE came a satyr creeping through the wood,
His hair fell on his breast, his legs were slim:
His eyes were dancing wickedly, he stood,
He peeped about on every side of him.

He danced! He peeped! But, at a sound I made,
A crackling twig, he turned; and, suddenly,
In three great jumps, he bounded to the shade,
And disappeared among the greenery!

James Stephens

Index of Poets and Titles